Scissor Skills
- dinosaur -

A Preschool Workbook For Kids

THIS BOOK BELONGS TO :

✂ _____

_____ ✂

Learning the Art and Skills of Using Scissor

Have we ever thought that when we should introduce our kids to use scissors?
It should be way earlier than we think.

Cutting involves our both hands doing different job and which requires practice. Our main hand holds the scissor and other hand holds the paper.

It requires the ability to use fingers, thumb, and balance to function accurately.

Therefore, it can harm those who don't know how to use it especially children. Hence, children need to establish skills which come through practice.

However, learning to use scissor carefully is an important skill especially for children. It can be danger for those who don't know how to use it as its blades are very sharp.

As children use it in schools as well, therefore, parents, elders and teachers should educate and guide them how to use scissor so that they can develop their skills.

For children, scissor should only be use for cutting papers and that is all.

Why Scissor Skills is Important?

Key notes:

1. It can cut papers accurately and reduce human efforts.
2. It can strengthen our hands muscles.
3. Scissors can enhance our focus and can also develop the hand-eye coordination.

Teaching the use of scissors to children can be frustrating for parents or teachers but it is very essential for their safety.

Tips:

Hold scissors properly:
- Train your kids to make use of scissors only to cut papers in onwards direction and off from body.

Hold scissor in correct manner:
- Teach your child the most appropriate way to hold the scissor.

Pass scissor carefully:
- Ask your child to give scissor carefully and do not throw it. Moreover, not to walk having scissor in hands.

Hence, it does not matter how long it takes to learn but what matter is the right and careful use of scissor.

Cutting Practice

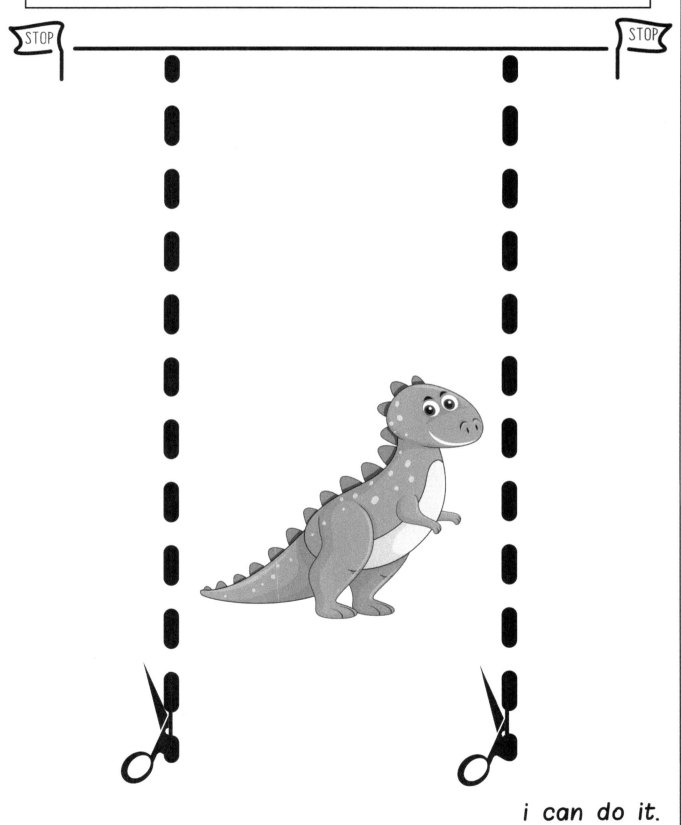

i can do it.

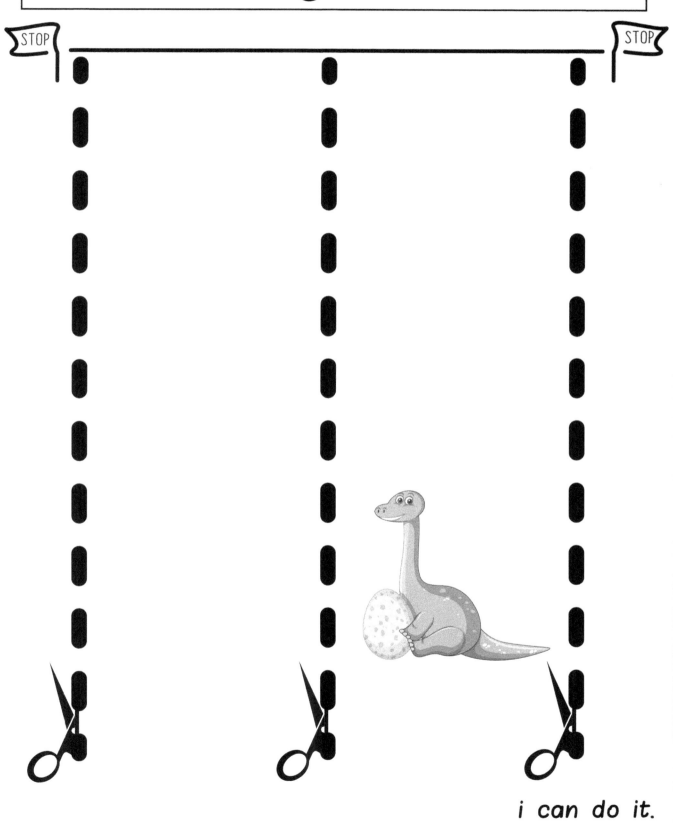

Cutting Practice

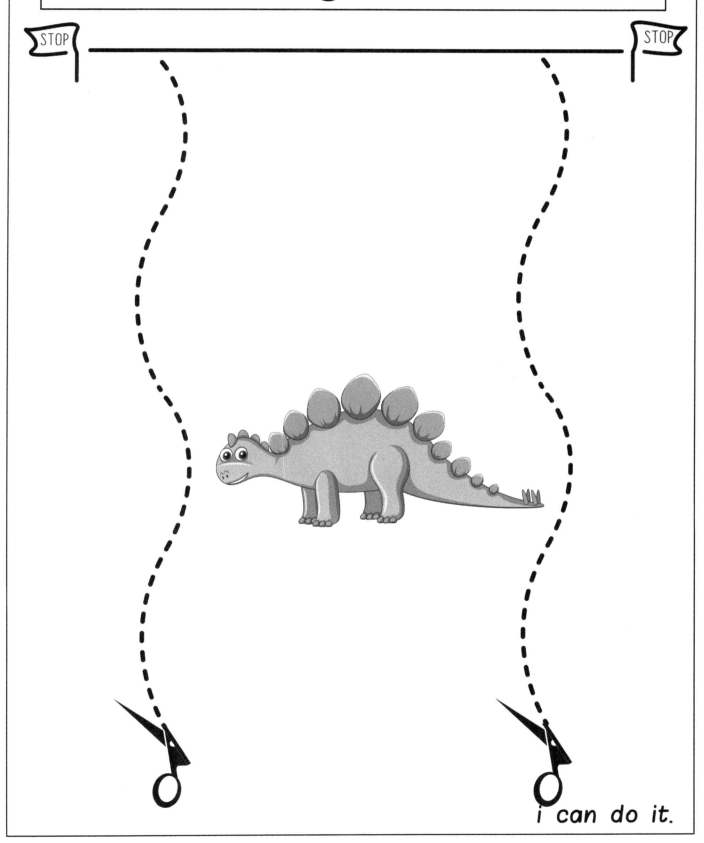

i can do it.

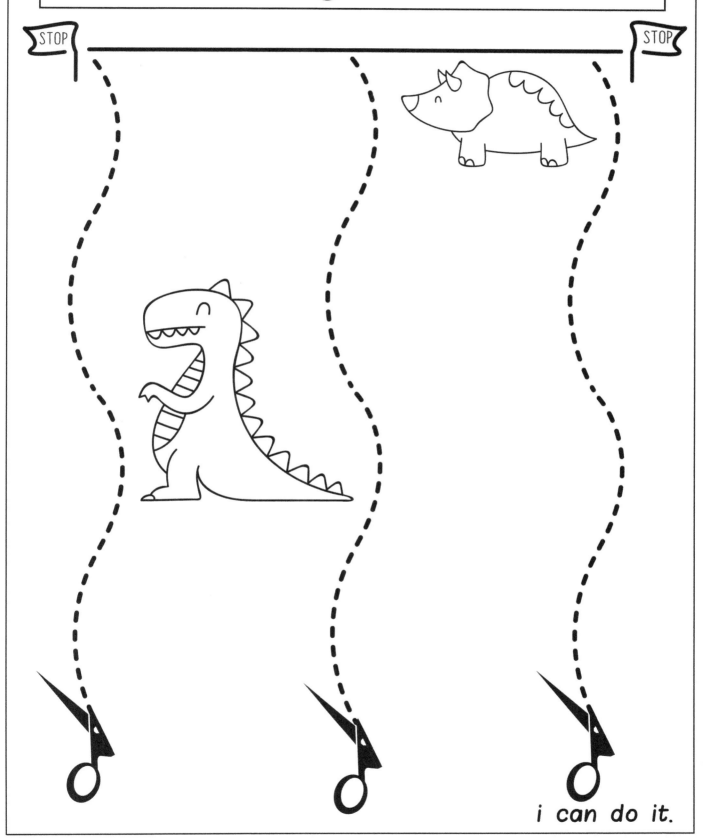

Cutting Practice

i can do it.

Cutting Practice

i can do it.

Cutting Practice

i can do it.

Cutting Practice

STOP　　　　　　　　　　　　　STOP

i can do it.

Cutting Practice

STOP　　　STOP

i can do it.

Cutting Practice

i can do it.

Cutting Practice

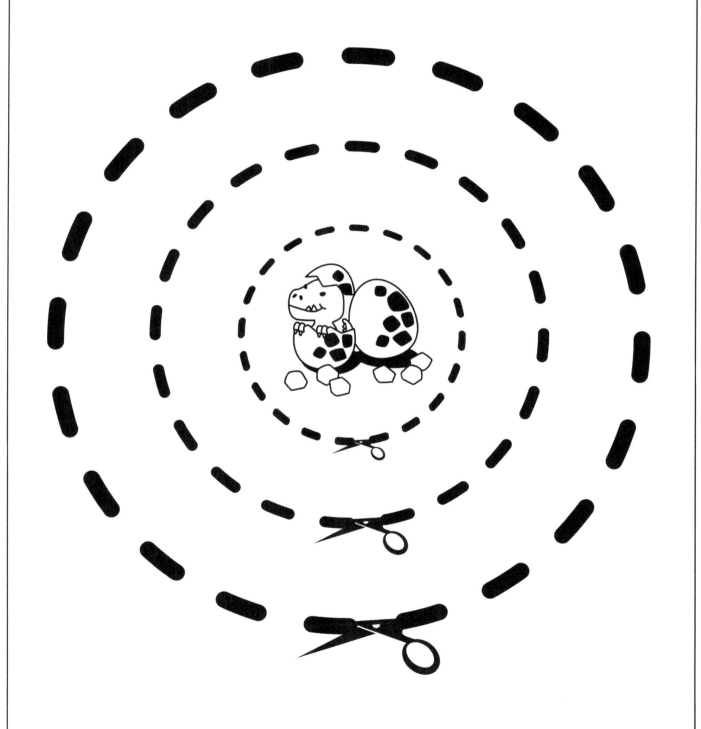

i can do it.

let's cut it.

i can do it.

let's cut it.

i can do it.

let's cut it.

i can do it.

Let's cut it.

i can do it.

Let's cut it.

i can do it.

let's cut it.

i can do it.

let's cut it.

i can do it.

Let's cut it.

i can do it.

let's cut it.

i can do it.

let's cut it.

i can do it.

Let's cut it.

i can do it.

let's cut it.

i can do it.

let's cut it.

i can do it.

Let's cut it.

i can do it.

let's cut it.

i can do it.

Let's cut it.

i can do it.

Let's cut it.

i can do it.

let's cut it.

i can do it.

let's cut it.

i can do it.

Let's cut it.

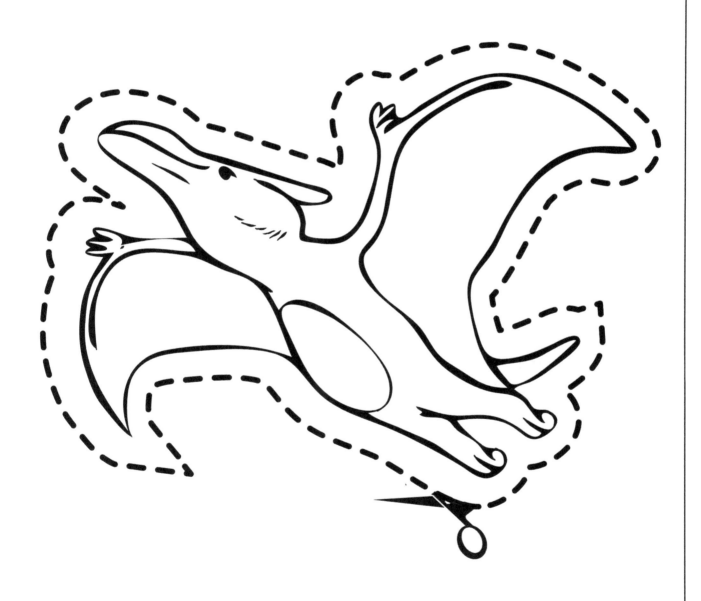

i can do it.

let's cut it.

i can do it.

Let's cut it.

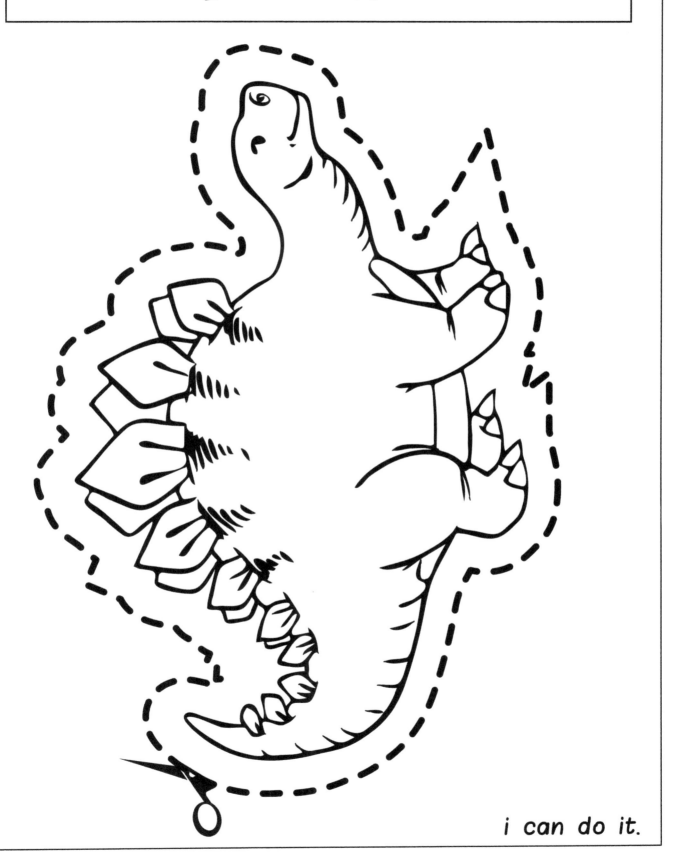

i can do it.

let's cut it.

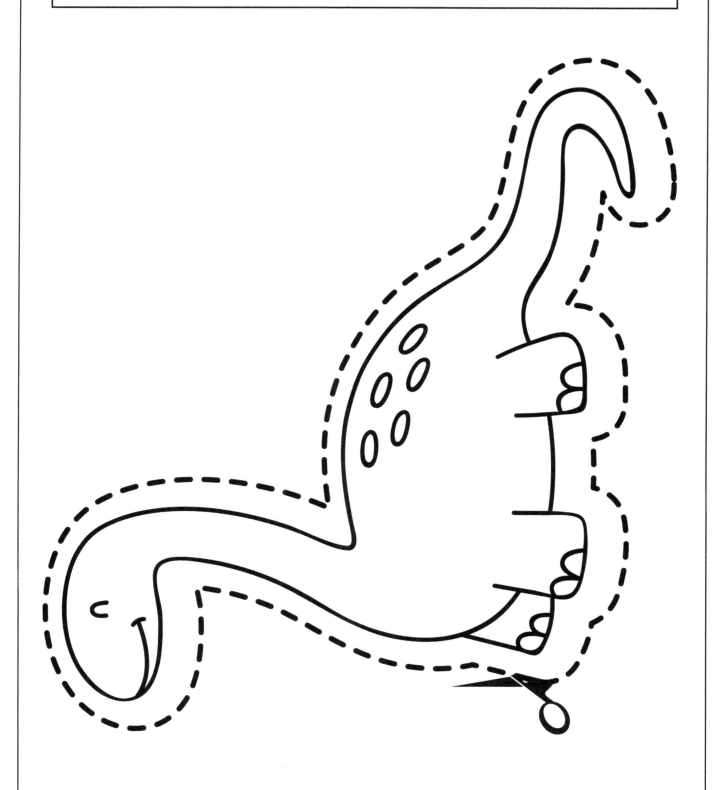

i can do it.

let's cut it.

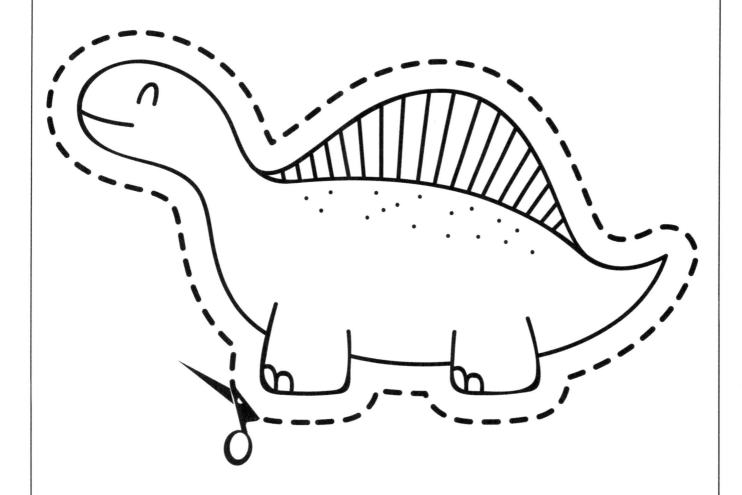

i can do it.

Let's cut it.

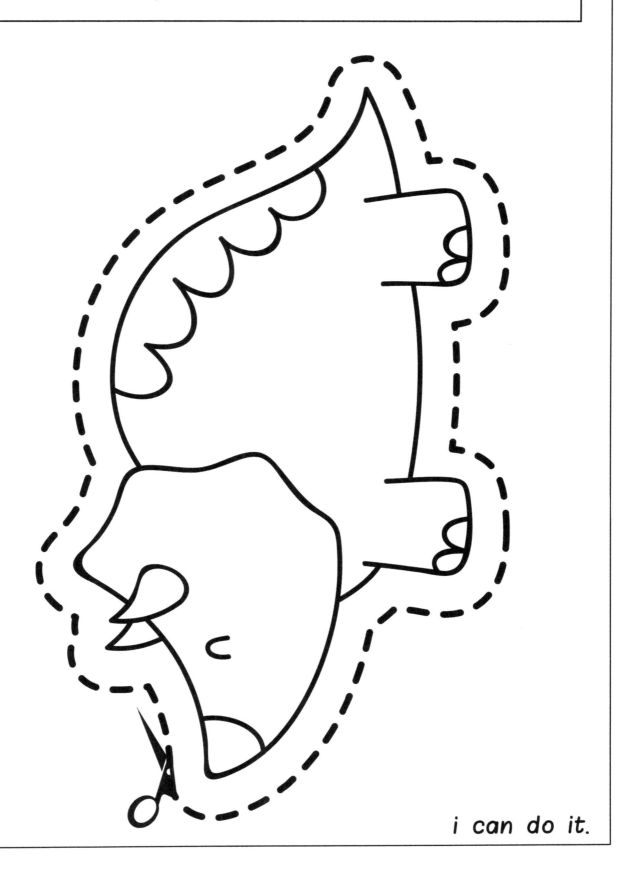

i can do it.

Let's cut it.

i can do it.

let's cut it.

i can do it.

Let's cut it.

i can do it.

Let's cut it.

i can do it.

let's cut it.

i can do it.

Let's cut it.

i can do it.

Let's cut it.

i can do it.

let's cut it.

i can do it.

Let's cut it.

i can do it.

Let's cut it.

i can do it.

Let's cut it.

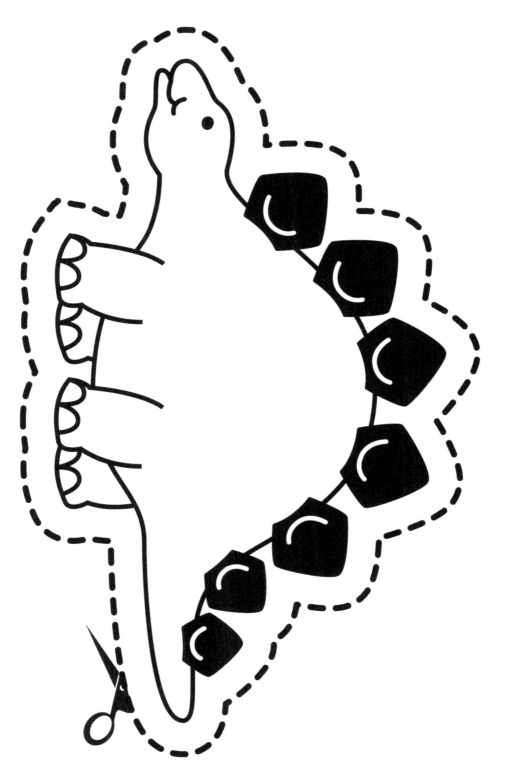

i can do it.

let's cut it.

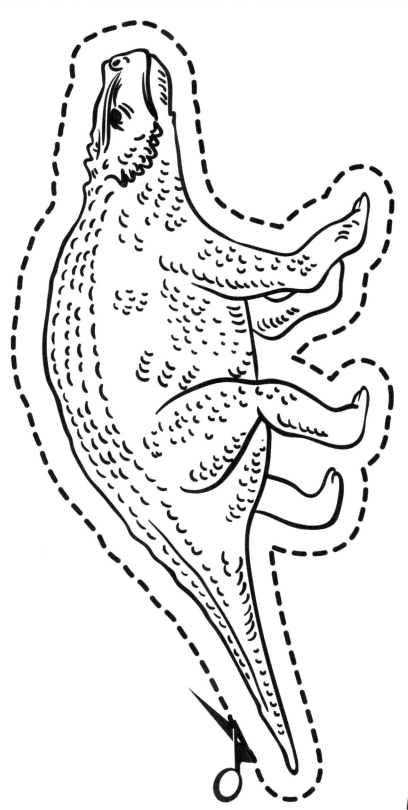

i can do it.

let's cut it.

i can do it.

Let's cut it.

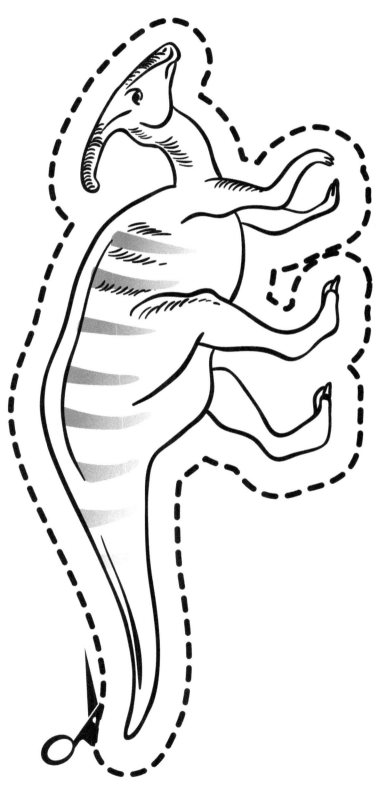

i can do it.

CPSIA information can be obtained
at www.ICGtesting.com
Printed in the USA
LVHW020729240623
750698LV00037B/990